I0086406

And She Called Him Lord

Wendy L. Magee

Foreword by David Magee Jr.

i

And She Called Him Lord
Copyright © 2015 Wendy L. Magee
www.wendymagee.org

Printed in United States of America. All rights reserved. No part of this book may be reproduced or transmitted in any form or by any means without written permission from the author.

Unless otherwise indicated, all Scripture quotations are from Blue Letter Bible www.blueletterbible.org and You Version Bible Application www.blible.com.

I would like to acknowledge the editorial services provided by Melinda Morris, professional copy editor. Thank you for your assistance with this project.

I would also like to acknowledge the cover design by Kirk Batiste. You have been a blessing to my family, and I really appreciate you.

Special thanks to my sister, Clarita Vaughn; my friend, Maria Hamilton; and First Lady at Evangelistic Ministry Church, Dr. Cynthia Bolden, for their guidance.

ARROW PUBLISHING

ISBN-13: 978-0692594803
ISBN-10: 0692594809

Dedication

I dedicate this book to my husband, David Magee Jr. I am so honored to have you as my husband. You are the lord of our home, and I thank you for your patience, love, and guidance.

Contents

FOREWORD

This book will encourage husbands to live their lives in such a way that their wives have no problem calling them Lord. Wives will call their husband Lord as a sign of validation for his role in the family and respect for the responsibility God has given him. After reading this book, it should be the prayer of every husband that his wife understands that her submission is a reflection of her appreciation of his role as a leader and how she genuinely feels in her heart and not out of fear or a perceived obligation. A preacher named Jack Taylor said, "Almighty God has mandated that every man bring his wife to the splendor of Jesus Christ." Husbands should create an atmosphere conducive for submission in love without fear. When our families start to function as God created, we will live a life of peace beyond understanding, compelling the world to investigate the power of God for a divorce-proof marriage.

-David Magee Jr

Introduction

This journey began on August 22, 2015, the last night of the Franklin Avenue marriage retreat in Destin, Fla. This was the third year for David and I attended, and we enjoyed the benefits of being around other Christian couples. Every year on the last night, the pastors hold a renewing-of-vows ceremony. This year, before the vows ceremony, a couple was tasked with reading a poem. The young man was reading to his wife, and his wife did the same. As I listened to the young lady read, it was very inspiring until she ended with saying, "And I will call you Lord."

My facial expression told it all. I enjoyed the poem, but could not wrap my thoughts around calling my husband, "Lord." David looked at me and asked, "Will you call me Lord?" No response, but I thought, *"Why should I if he does not deserve the title. Should my children call him Lord too?"*

On the drive home with my in-laws, the question was asked again, and my mother-in-law had some of the same questions I had thought to myself. It was never answered well enough for me to have a change of heart.

On August 29, 2015, David and I, along with some church members, went to see the movie "War Room." The movie touched me so much that I found myself journaling, which I haven't done in over five years. I started reading and studying the "War Room" devotion on my Bible app. The devotion put me back into a place where I felt as if I were back in right order with God concerning my prayer life. I had recently been asking God to help me balance being a wife, mother, and full-time worker. God *always* answers your prayers.

On September 4, 2015, as I was studying, I came across a Scripture David had highlighted. It was 1 Peter 3 Amplified. As I read, God began to reveal the true purpose of a wife and why Sarah called Abraham "Lord."

1 Peter 3:1-9 (Amplified)

In the same way, you wives, be submissive to your own husbands [subordinate, not as inferior, but out of respect for the responsibilities entrusted to husbands and their accountability to God, and so partnering with them] so that even if some do not obey the word [of God], they may be won over [to Christ] without discussion by the *godly* lives of their wives, ² when they see your modest and respectful behavior [together with your devotion and appreciation—love your husband, encourage him, and enjoy him as a blessing from God]. ³ Your adornment must not be *merely* external—with interweaving *and* elaborate knotting of the hair, and wearing gold jewelry, or [being superficially preoccupied with] dressing in *expensive* clothes; ⁴ but let it be [the inner beauty of] the hidden person of the heart, with the imperishable quality *and* unfading charm of a gentle and peaceful spirit, [one that is calm and self-controlled, not overanxious, but serene and spiritually mature] which is very precious in the sight of God. [5] For in this way in former times the holy women, who hoped in God, used to adorn themselves, being submissive to their own husbands *and* adapting themselves to them; [6] just as Sarah obeyed Abraham [following him and having regard for him as head of their house], calling him lord. And you have become her daughters if you do what is right without being frightened by any fear [that is, being respectful toward your husband but not giving in to intimidation, nor allowing yourself to be led into sin, nor to be harmed].

[7] In the same way, you husbands, live with *your wives* in an understanding way [with great gentleness and tact, and with an intelligent regard for the marriage relationship], as with someone physically weaker, since she is a woman. Show her honor *and* respect as a fellow heir of the grace of life, so that your prayers will not be hindered *or* ineffective.

[8] Finally, all of you be like-minded [united in spirit], sympathetic, brotherly, kindhearted

[courteous and compassionate toward each other as members of one household], and humble in spirit; [9] and never return evil for evil or insult for insult [avoid scolding, berating, and any kind of abuse], but on the contrary, give a blessing [pray for one another's well-being, contentment, and protection]; for you have been called for this very purpose, that you might inherit a blessing [from God that brings well-being, happiness, and protection].

That night around 3 a.m., God had me share with David my thoughts on 1 Peter 3. God had revealed to me the true meaning of our roles and responsibilities as husband and wife. Knowing who you are in Christ, and God's order of the family, even *before* you consider marriage, is an important key to understanding why you should reverence your husband as lord.

> Actions don't change just
> position

Like a virgin (unwed woman), you do the things of the Lord. As a married woman, you care for the things of your home. Couples must understand that Christ never ceases to be Lord over your lives as you transition into marriage. Actions don't change just position. Marriage has been designed by God for the world to see a picture of Christ's relationship with His Church. The way a wife treats her husband is an overflow of our relationship with God.

As a single woman, you have the power to accept his hand in marriage. Afterward, you forfeit your singleness to the mission of your husband.

The purpose of this book is to encourage married couples to grow closer and experience life without arguments and to have the love of God that will, in turn, enhance intimacy in your home.

For single people, as you are preparing yourself for marriage, this book is also a guide. As a Christian single, you have to know who you are in Christ before embarking marriage.

This book will be your marriage roadmap to making sound and godly choices. In the end, let the peace of God rule your heart.

After reading each chapter, you will be given the opportunity to write a purposeful prayer. Each prayer is to come from your heart and to be in you. Following the prayer, you will be challenged to do or think differently.

> And let the peace of God rule in your hearts, to the which also ye are called in one body; and be ye thankful.
>
> -Colossians 3:15

Chapter One

⟨℘⟩

Submission is a Command

"Sometimes to submit is to know you have a life worth living for a higher purpose, worth seeing through." [1]
—*A. J. Darkholme*

I recognize the topic of submission is not widely spoken about among women. I do believe the term has become misinterpreted, and many people have stop viewing marriage as God intended. The word submission means "the state of being obedient; the act of accepting the authority or control of someone else." [2]

> Root word Sub: to come under

A wife being submissive to her *own* husband is not for her husband's good behavior, but a command of God. A godly wife will submit to her husband as unto the Lord because she understands the purpose and meaning of God's order. Understanding the true meaning of a word, along with the guidance of the Holy Spirit, opened my eyes. The root words of submission are sub, "to come under," and mission, "a task or job that someone is given to do." As a single man you should seek God on the purpose and the mission God has for him. Single women should prepare by submitting to God's word. In courtship, women should know what the man's mission and purpose are before accepting his hand in marriage.

Submission is not to be used for the husband to dictate to his wife and children or for the wife to feel less valued. It is an order that God has set in place. It's a leadership position that is to be respected and honored.

RESPECT THE POSITION

Being married for eight years has been wonderful, but having a clearer understanding of submitting would have made things smoother.

> …Wives should submit to their
> husbands in everything.

As a single woman, learning this concept is part of your preparation. Dreaming of a huge wedding is great, but if you are not preparing yourself for submission, it will be hard to respect the position.

Wives, submit to your husbands as to the Lord. For the husband is the head of the wife as Christ is the head of the Church, his body, of which he is the Savior. Now as the Church submits to Christ, so also wives should submit to their husbands in everything.

-Ephesians 5:22

My husband asked the question "*If you respect the role of your pastor, would you argue with him?*" The reason arguments occur in marriage is due to the lack of respect for that person's position. If you, as a wife, trust God, and honor the position God has set, then no arguments should take place in the home.

NOT ONLY IN ACTIONS

Submission is easily spoken about but rarely put into action. If your heart is willing, it will be easy. If you love God, it will show through your obedience in your marriage. Wives display the role of the church by loving their husbands as the head of the house, who submits to Christ, who is the head of the Church.

For as he thinks in his heart, so is he. As one who reckons, he says to you, eat and drink, yet his heart is not with you [but is grudging the cost].
-Proverbs 23:7

Our lifestyles testify to what we believe. As a wife, or if you are in preparation, submission is a lifestyle. When you begin to fix it in your heart, that submission is an order with equality in importance, dignity, and honor, it will be more than just an action or task, but a lifestyle that can be replicated and made an example to younger women.

Submission is a lifestyle

Then they [the older women] can train the younger women to love their husband and children, to be self-controlled and pure, to be busy at home, to be kind and subject to their husband, so that no one will malign the Word of God.

-Titus 2:4-5

SHIFTING YOUR PERSPECTIVE

Changing your perspective is a valuable tool to better understand a situation and help to avoid false views. The simplest way is to view situations from every position. This will allow you to see things that were hidden in another position. [3]

God has given us instruction describing the *one* true meaning of marriage. Whether you are single, engaged, married for one year or ten years, it's never too late for you to seek God's wisdom.

FOLLOW HIS LEAD

As a child, I played follow the leader. The purpose of this game was to listen to the directions of the leader and to trust that the person will lead you and not allow you to fall.

David often asked, *"Do you trust me to lead?"* My mouth quickly answered, "yes," but my actions showed differently. When you decide to be totally submissive in actions and heart, you are showing God you trust him and will hold God to his word concerning your husband's actions.

> Experience intimacy on
> another level

....From everyone to whom much has been given, much will be required; and to whom they entrusted much, of him they will ask all the more.

-Luke 12:48

Leading is not easy, and requires a lot of responsibility. As a wife, praying for your husband is vital. God designed man to be able to handle the leadership role. Women are emotional beings, which is a great characteristic for raising children and tending to the home, but not for leading as God intended.

Being able to follow his lead and trust the decisions being made for the family is God's perfect order. A godly man will consider his wife concerning decisions, but if he doesn't, don't be angry--*TRUST*.

FOCUSING ON THE POSITIVE

Having positive thoughts is not only what God has instructed but also practical to healthy living. The Bible contains many scriptures on thoughts and the mind:

Finally, brethren, whatsoever things are true, whatsoever things are honest, whatsoever things are just, whatsoever things are pure, whatsoever things are lovely, whatsoever things are of good report; if there be any virtue, and if there be any praise, think on these things.

-Philippians 4:8

A joyful heart is good medicine, but a crushed spirit dries up the bones.

-Proverbs 17:22

You keep him in perfect peace whose mind is stayed on you because he trusts in you.

-Isaiah 26:3

Think on these things, and it will become you. Trust in God's Word, and it will live in you. Think positive thoughts, give positive praises to your spouse, and they will become the person you have grown to love through Christ Jesus.

DIG DEEP

1. Do you consider yourself to be submissive?_____

   _____

2. What challenges are you having that keep you from submitting?

   _____

   _____

3. What are some things you can do to show your appreciation?

   _____

   _____

4. Do you pray for and with your spouse?_____

   _____

5. Do you believe your husband to be a leader?_____

   _____

PERSONAL PRAYER

Write a prayer to help with understanding the power of submission.

_____

_____

_____

_____

_____

_____

_____

_____

_____

_____

_____

_____

_____

_____

TO DO:

1. Do something special for your spouse.
2. Practice having a different response to difficult situations.

Chapter Two

⟨℘⟩

Win Without Words

Winning is a habit. Watch your thoughts. They become your beliefs. Watch your beliefs. They become your words. Watch your words. They become your actions.
—Vince Lombardi

Being submissive can be the most powerful tool you have as a woman. It has all the benefits, and will affect your husband in such a way that he will withhold no good thing from you as God would his obedient children.

…So that even if any do not obey the Word [of God], they may be won over not by discussion but by the [godly] lives of their wives

1 Peter 3:1 Amplified

MEEKNESS

A wife's submission shows her trust in God. As a single woman who served God and did the things as unto God, she has to transition that service to her husband.

Emotional control can accomplish new heights in marriage. A good friend's son, who is only four years old, defined meekness as "strength under control." When a woman is meek and humble, she is the most influential person in her husband's life. Meekness is *not* a weakness of character, but a strength of it. It requires great self-control to submit to others.[2]

Meekness is one of the fruits of the Spirit-qualities that we must possess if we are led by the Spirit.

-Galatians 5:22-23

> Meekness is *not* a weakness of character

Part of being submissive is being humble. Reading Andrew Murray's book "*Humility*" showed me how pride can be in my heart without me even noticing. Pride is the opposite of humility and not pleasing to God. Humility, the place of total dependence on God, is from the very nature of things, the first duty, the highest virtue of a person, and the root of every virtue.

Having this mind in you which was also in Christ Jesus:
emptied Himself; taking the form of a servant, and
humbled Himself; becoming obedient even unto death.
Wherefore God also highly exalted him.

-Philippians 2:5-9

Jesus "emptied himself" simply means he contained nothing; his purpose was not his own, but what God purposed for him. If you are empty, it's not your purpose or will, but God. In marriage, both the husband and the wife have to be emptied. The wife being submissive to her husband; the husband, to God.

POWER OF THE TONGUE

As husband and wife, the way you communicate to each other is vital in your marriage. Before our wedding day, married couples often told us that communication is the key.

The tongue has the power of life and death, and those
who love it will eat its fruit.

-Proverbs 18:21

What you say to your spouse and how you say it could cause him to react positively or negatively. To avoid arguments, figure out the best way to communicate with your spouse. My husband and I read the book "*Five Love Languages.*" It benefited us greatly knowing how we respond to different situations.

> Communication is Key

Not only is communicating to each other important, but maintaining a consistent communication with God together as a family, and personally, is vital to any marriage. When I begin to get short-tempered, my husband often asks *"When was the last time you read your devotion or studied?"* He is not asking to start an argument but to keep me accountable.

A wife can get consumed with children and other duties of the home that in some cases can place spending time with God on the back burner. It is important that collectively you and your hold each other accountable to the Word of God.

My father-in-law said, *"If you find yourself arguing with your spouse, then you are not spending enough time with each other."* Just as not spending enough time with God creates an imbalance within you, the same holds true with your spouse. Spending time with each other and having open dialogues consistently will eliminate assumptions, misunderstandings, and negative communications.

I have been blessed to see good examples of other Christian couples. My husband and I learn from each other and have real conversations about how to grow in marriage and with each other. Becoming one doesn't happen overnight, but surrounding yourself with like-minded people will steer you in the right direction.

EXPRESSIONS

In 1986, Janet Jackson came out with a song called *"What have you done for me lately?"* After reading the lyrics, I realized it was all about what the man used to do for her, but things changed. In truth, marriage is not about what your spouse has done for you but what have you done to be of service to them. When was the last time you expressed how you felt about your spouse? When was the last time you said something that added to his life? A lot of times, I find that people may have positive thoughts or want to encourage their spouse, but never tell them. They would rather stay angry than look for the good in them.

An expression is making someone know your feelings. In marriage, being able to express yourself to your spouse is important and should be welcomed. If you feel offended by something your spouse did, pray, and allow God to correct them. I have learned to listen to the Holy Spirit on matters of the heart. The Holy Spirit will tell you when to speak up or shut up. Trust me, it's best to listen. If you believe your spouse to hear from God, they will come back and make it right. When you decide to override the Holy Spirit, it will not go well, as your spouse will not receive it from you like he would from God.

Find opportunities to say something kind to your spouse. A lot of times we get caught up in technology and electronics that we forget the basics. Handwrite them a letter or allow space for them to do the things they enjoy. My husband enjoys basketball, and I, volleyball. We have certain days of the week that we get to enjoy these activities. If it's watching football, HGTV, or the Cooking Network, let your spouse enjoy that time, in fact, join in and enjoy it as a couple.

LOVE MATTERS

In marriage, love matters. There are many passages in the Bible that talks about love:

Love is patient and kind; love does not envy or boast; it is not arrogant or rude. It does not insist on its own way; it is not irritable or resentful; it does not rejoice at wrongdoing, but rejoices with the truth. Love bears all things, believes all things, hopes all things, endures all things. Love never ends. As for prophecies, they will pass away; as for tongues, they will cease; as for knowledge, it will pass away.

                              -1 Corinthians 13:4-8

With all humility and gentleness, with patience, bearing with one another in love, eager to maintain the unity of the Spirit in the bond of peace.

                              - Ephesians 4:2-3

Complete my joy by being of the same mind, having the same love, being in full accord and of one mind.

                              - Philippians 2:2

Beyond all these things put on love, which is the perfect bond of unity.

                              -Colossians 3:14

Love covers, it protects, and it causes a perfect bond in unity. Perfect is absolute; it's complete. When you love each other, you will protect your marriage. The husband will cover his wife, but the key is that she has to get under his covering. The husband also has to have his family under the covering of their pastor. Submission is part of the order, and when you are in order, God begins to bless your marriage.

DIG DEEP

1. Are you winning without words?

   _____

   _____

2. What challenges are you having expressing yourself?

   _____

   _____

3. What are some characteristics of your spouse that you love?

   _____

   _____

4. What activities does your spouse enjoy?

   _____

   _____

5. What are some positive words you can use to lift and encourage your spouse?

   _____

   _____

   _____

PERSONAL PRAYER

Write a prayer to give you guidance on how to win without words.

_____

_____

_____

_____

_____

_____

_____

_____

_____

_____

_____

_____

_____

_____

TO DO:

1. Hand write a letter to your spouse.
2. Spend time with your spouse doing one of his favorite activities.

Chapter Three

$\mathcal{P}$

True Beauty of a Godly Woman

*The beauty of a woman is not in a facial mode, but the true
beauty in a woman is reflected in her soul.*
-Audrey Hepburn

Why do women allow society to dictate to
them their definition of beauty? It is not true
that beauty is only skin deep, If your heart is
hard, and your attitude is negative, that's not
true beauty.

But the Lord said to Samuel, "Do not consider his
appearance or his height, for I have rejected him.
The Lord does not look at the things people look at.
People look at the outward appearance, but
the Lord looks at the heart."
-1 Samuel 16:7

WHO ARE YOU
In college, I believed that being in a
sorority was going to make me popular, make

me somebody. Little did I know that I didn't need letters on my chest to define me, or to show people I was pretty. Inner beauty doesn't change.

Let not yours be the [merely] external adorning with [elaborate] interweaving and knotting of the hair, the wearing of jewelry, or changes of clothes, But let it be the inward adorning and beauty of the hidden person of the heart, with the incorruptible and unfading charm of a gentle and peaceful spirit, which [is not anxious or wrought up, but] is very precious in the sight of God.
-1 Peter 3:3-4 Amplified

Now you are probably thinking, what does this have to do with submission? When women submit to their husbands and when they do not put their trust in their outward adornment, they are like the holy women, where they powerfully demonstrate their faith.[2]

Using your ability to change or control your spouse will never work. Why do people believe they can change people? *You* cannot change anyone. If you are married to an unbeliever, allow your life and quiet spirit to win them over through godly conduct.

Are you living a life guided by the Holy Spirit? Or are you pretending to be someone else? God wants you to be yourself. You should not have to go to the extreme to capture the attention of a person. Loving the person God has created, and knowing your purpose will allow you to be content in your singleness and in your marriage.

Not that I am implying that I was in any personal want, for I have learned how to be content (satisfied to the point where I am not disturbed or disquieted) in whatever state I am.

-Philippians 4:11 Amplified

Are you satisfied with your singleness and your marriage? God is the only person who truly knows your heart.

PURITY

People often associate purity with a person's virginity. What does it mean to be pure? Purity is the lack of guilt or evil thoughts. I was attending a Bible study at good friend's church, and he made this statement: *Purity is a heart condition.* If your heart is pure, your beauty will show, and bring you closer to your spouse.

Even in your singleness, exemplifying purity will attract a like spirit person. Operating outside the spirit, or desiring ungodly things, will attract those types of spirits. You will then be wondering why you continue to date ungodly people, or married someone to whom you are unequally yoked.

Purity is a heart condition

He who loves purity and the pure in heart and who is gracious in speech because of the grace of his lips will have the king for a friend.

-Proverbs 22:11 Amplified

Let your garments be always white [with purity], and let your head not lack [the] oil [of gladness].

-Ecclesiastes 9:8 Amplified

Let no one despise or think less of you because of your
youth, but be an example (pattern) for the believers in
speech, in conduct, in love, in faith, and in purity.
                                              -I Timothy 4:12 Amplified

QUIET SPIRIT

When I think of a quiet spirit, I think about
one of my friends. She is an example of a godly
wife and mother to her children. She is
submissive and listens to the Holy Spirit. She
has a beautiful spirit and allows her husband to
lead her. I think of myself as a person who
doesn't mind dealing with confrontation. Is this
godly?

But the fruit of the Spirit is love, joy peace,
longsuffering, gentleness, goodness, faith.
                                              -Galatians 5:22

Be ye angry, and sin not: let not the sun go down upon
your wrath: Neither give place to the devil.
                                              -Ephesians 4: 26, 27

Is it okay to get angry? Yes, but how do you handle it? Do you curse at people, belittle them? I'm learning that it's okay to deal with confrontation, but seeking my husband's advice and yielding to the Holy Spirit allows me to grow and handle my emotions. It also allows the other person to see the light and gives grace. If you want to reap grace, you must first sow.

God wants us to yield the fruits of the spirit. When we commit to these things, we are in fact showing great beauty in God's eyes. I'm not saying to neglect your physical features. I enjoy going to the hair salon, nail shop, and even the gym. It should be to honor and glorify God, not one's self.

This is an ongoing process. Seeking God through prayer will allow yourself to be cultivated until it becomes a godly habit. You want to be an example in your speech, attire, outward appearance, conduct, and etiquette. Remember people are watching you, and you want to point them in the right direction that leads them to Christ.

DIG DEEP

1. Are you living a lifestyle that reflects your inner beauty? _____

   _____

   _____

2. Are there tangible things that you believe enhance your beauty?

   _____

   _____

3. How do you protect your purity?

   _____

   _____

4. What are some ways you can remain pure?_____

   _____

5. How can you develop a pure mind?

   _____

   _____

   _____

PERSONAL PRAYER

Write a prayer on how you can be cultivated in the fruits of the spirit.

_____

_____

_____

_____

_____

_____

_____

_____

_____

_____

_____

_____

_____

TO DO:

1. Consider how the way you dress and speak demonstrate your inner values. Are you cultivating the fruits in other people? Write down some of your thoughts.

Chapter Four

∞

Sarah Obeyed Abraham

Obedience brings peace in decision making.[1]

-James E. Faust

While preparing to write this book, my mother-in-law offered me the book, *Me? Obey Him?* A few months before, I was saying the same thing. The revelation God has given me on submission has been life-changing.

OBEDIENCE

Obedience is *dutiful or submissive compliance to the commands of one in authority*. It is our duty to obey God, and yielding our wills to him. We have to remember that we don't obey God solely out of duty, but love.

Jesus answered and said unto him, If a man love me, he will keep my words: and my Father will love him,

and we will come unto him, and make our abode with
him.

-John 14:23

Also, understand that the spirit of obedience
is as important as the act of obedience. We
serve the Lord in humility, singleness of the
heart, and love.[2]

WHAT IF?

Planning a wedding could be stressful if
you allowed it. There are many things that can
and will go wrong, even with the best planners.
When you plan for marriage, life becomes
simple. Thinking about finances, housing, and
children after the honeymoon is a little late.
Sometimes because you fail to plan, the person
you wake up to the day after the wedding has
changed.

What if that person doesn't have a
relationship with God? That means he/she
doesn't have the conviction of the Holy Spirit.
What if…? Do you complain to God as Adam

and say *you gave me this woman?* Or do you begin to allow God to reveal himself to you?

In I Samuel 25, there you will find a story about a woman whose obedience saved her entire household. Abigail is a woman of good understanding and beautiful appearance. Her husband, Nabal, who was a wealthy man, was harsh and evil in his doings. During the traditional harvest and sheep shearing time, David requests compensation from Nabal for protecting his flock. Nabal refused payment. As a result, David ordered his men to kill all the males in the household. A servant overheard Nabal's refusal and went to Abigail. Instead of her badmouthing her husband, she quickly acted and gathered the finest food and presented to David. He received from her and said, *"go up in peace to your house. See, I have heeded your voice and respected your person."*

As a wife, you have to be able to hear from God. Women frequently ask me *What if* questions. I cannot base my life on the *ifs*; I

have to trust that the man I married can hear
from God, and if he makes the wrong decision
concerning the house, God will convict him.
There are no IFS with God.

If you can? Said Jesus, "Everything is possible for one
who believes
-Mark 9:23 NIV

The "if" is not with God, but man. I have
seen God speak to my husband, and he has
come back to me and changed the decision.
Jesus is our advocate. Allow him to go to God
on our behalf. It is critical that you know who
you are marrying. God gives you signs. You
have to be able to separate emotion, and make a
sound decision. Marriage is a business decision.
Your husband is your partner, your teammate,
and you have to know with whom you are
going into business. Why settle for if, when you
can have all?

Marriage was created and intentionally
designed by God primarily to show a dying
world what the relationship between Christ and

His bride (the Church) should look like. In marriage, we become one and there should be no room for any breaches. It is a three-way covenant, a covenant between man and wife and most importantly, God.

> There are no IFS with God

INTIMACY

In marriage, obedience also comes in the form of intimacy. Intimacy is a closeness between two people. Intimacy can be obtained as the husband and wife seek to unconditionally love each other by fulfilling each other's needs within the marriage. Each husband and wife team is made up of two large puzzle pieces, that when fit together, will create a beautiful panoramic picture of what marital intimacy is all about.[3]

One might wonder, what does obedience have to do with intimacy?

Let the husband render unto the wife due benevolence: and likewise also the wife unto the husband. The wife hath no power of her own body, but the husband: and likewise also the husband hath no power of his own body, but the wife. Defraud ye not one the other, except it be with consent for a time...

-1 Corinthians 7:3-5

As husband and wife, sex should not be used against one another as punishment. Disobedience comes when one person intentionally denies sex from their spouse. The Bible states "render what is due.'' Not just speaking to the woman, but also to the man. As a mother of two, and having a full-time job, I understand being tired at times. Even at my weakest points, I find comfort in knowing my husband wants to be intimate with me. Why would I forfeit that time with him, or create separation in our oneness by denying him?

Can two walk together, except they be agreed?

-Amos 3:3

For this reason a man shall leave his father and his mother and shall be joined to his wife, and the two shall become one flesh. [Gen. 2: 24.]

-Ephesians 4:31

So they are no longer two, but one flesh. What therefore God has joined together, let not man put asunder (separate).

-Matthew 19:6

Becoming one flesh is a work in progress. Constant communication with your spouse, praying together, being intimate with each other, and allowing God to be the final authority will allow your marriage to be an example of Christ in the Church.

DIG DEEP

1. What is your understanding of obedience?_____

_____

_____

2. Do you have *what ifs*?

_____

_____

3. Are you willing to become one flesh?

_____

_____

4. How do you show your obedience to God in your marriage?

_____

_____

5. What things can you do or change in order for your marriage to be an example of Christ in the Church?

_____

_____

_____

PERSONAL PRAYER

Focus on obedience.

_____

_____

_____

_____

_____

_____

_____

_____

_____

_____

_____

_____

_____

TO DO:

1. Write some goals down with your spouse or fiancé on becoming one.
2. Hang it on your refrigerator and have weekly communication and prayer time with each other.

Chapter Five

Giving Honor to the Wife

No person was ever honored for what he received.
Honor has been the reward for what he gave.
-Calvin Coolidge

Early in my marriage, David and I would argue, and I would often threaten to leave. His response would be, "If you leave, it's because you made the decision, not me." He was committed to the vows we made to each other before God.

DWELL TOGETHER

As I was studying 1 Peter 3:7, it referenced a husband dwelling with his wife. What does it mean to dwell? To dwell means to hang in there; and your spouse is becoming a part of you.

So ought men to love their wives as their own bodies.
He that loveth his wife loveth himself.
-Ephesians 5:28

If you had known Me, you would have known My
Father also; from now on you know Him, and have seen
Him.

-John 14:7

If your husband honors you as his wife, he
would not be physically or mentally abusive.
To hear women in domestic violence
relationship say "I know he loves me when he
hits me" or "it doesn't happen all the time."
This abuse is not giving honor.

The fear of the LORD is the beginning of knowledge;
Fools despise wisdom and instruction.

-Proverbs 1:7

A husband that wants to honor his wife
wants to be around her, he wants to be one with
her. He will not abuse the submissive role of
the wife. He will respect, and value her. In
marriage, you are one unit, one voice
...univocal. If you are one, there is no
difference, no distinction between each other.

YOU UNDERSTAND ME?

I remember countless times arguing with David and telling him that he didn't understand me, or what I'd been through. When I pondered on those words, I realized it was me wanting to be the victim instead of listening to my husband. I wanted to make excuses for my actions.

1 Peter 3:7 goes on to say:

> Husbands, likewise, dwell with *them* with understanding, giving honor to the wife, as to the weaker vessel...

With the guidance of the Holy Spirit, the husband learns how to understand his wife. With understanding comes honor, with honor comes love. As a wife, if you believe your husband is not being understanding, then go to God. A godly husband is in constant communication with God. He is providing him with directives on how to lead his family. If he is listening, God will reveal to him if he is understanding.

As a woman, you should understand that when the Bible refers to us as the weaker vessel, it doesn't mean you are weak spiritually. It's referring to our stature. Men are built bigger and stronger than women. Because of this, godly husbands should handle his wife with care. When I read this passage, I think about mailing a package that is fragile. I wrap it to keep it from breaking and ensure the post office stamps it *handle with care.* Anybody handling this package will be delicate, and careful with it so the item won't break. It's the same with a wife. Husbands should handle their wife with care. He should cover and protect her from breaking spiritually.

God has given men the wisdom on how to handle his wife. The wife also has a responsibility to allow the husband to care for her. I know there are secular songs about women being independent. That's great if you are single and don't desire to be married. When you are married, you are one. No one is independent, but together as one.

IS YOUR HUSBAND ON THE ROOFTOP

It is better to live in a corner of a roof than in a house shared with a contentious woman.

-Proverbs 21:9

In marriage, it doesn't go *if he treats me this way, and then I will do this.* Regardless of how your spouse treats you, you will do your part. The husband should honor his wife even if she is not submissive. He should love her into submission. It should be so good, that she doesn't want to do anything but serve you.

As the wife, if you believe your husband is not honoring you, check your attitude and behavior. Are you speaking negatively? Are you disrespectful to him, especially in public? Being a contentious woman is not godly. You are embarrassing your husband, and you are not being an example of Christ in the church. Whether you like it or not, people are watching you as a wife and how are you handling situations. I know a lot of single women who are afraid to get married because of what

49

they have seen. When you are submissive, and he honors you, all people will see is oneness.

> Love her into submission

I remember watching the movie *War Room*. When the wife began her journey, she had doubts. She was eating, playing on her phone, and couldn't think clearly to get a prayer through. When she completely cleared out the closet, and began to lay before the Lord, he begins to reveal himself to her. It got to a point where the husband was baffled when she didn't argue back, and he couldn't do anything, but to honor and respect her.

Husbands, love your wives, even as Christ also loved the church, and gave himself for it.
For no man ever yet hated his own flesh; but nourisheth and cherisheth it, even as the Lord the church:
-Ephesians 5:25, 26

MARRIAGE IS AN INVESTMENT

Dating is often referred to as courtship. Courtship is two people having no physical contact with each other with the intentions to see if the other person is suitable for marriage. At this time, you are learning about this person, and understanding who they truly are.

Marriage is an investment. People worry about how to invest their money, or investing in their future, but what about your marriage? I read an article titled *5 Tips for Investing in your Wife.*

After reading the article, it revealed that my husband was in fact investing in me. He sees me as a participating partner by respecting my opinion. He protects me when I stay under the covering. He always honors me in public and behind closed doors. He has shown me that my administrative gifts are just as important as the people in the spotlight. Lastly, he is my buffer. When I need problems solved, I go to him especially when I get upset about something-to get godly advice on how to handle situations.

When you put in work to invest in your marriage, you will have an overflow of blessings. God will bless your entire household. You will see the payoff in your children, your job, and yourself. When you make a decision to commit fully to your marriage, God will begin to open doors and resolve issues that you thought could never be repaired.

DIG DEEP

1. How does your spouse honor you?

   _____

   _____

2. Are your actions preventing your spouse from dwelling with you?

   _____

   _____

3. Do you believe you can be contentious?_____

   _____

   _____

4. Is your husband on the rooftop?

   _____

   _____

5. Do you view marriage as an investment?_____

   _____

PERSONAL PRAYER
Write a prayer investing time into God.

_____

_____

_____

_____

_____

_____

_____

_____

_____

_____

_____

_____

_____

_____

TO DO:

1. Do something to honor your spouse.
2. With your spouse discuss ways to be univocal.

Chapter Six

Heirs Together

Coming together is a beginning; keeping together is progress; working together is success.

-Henry Ford

When I understood that my husband was on the same team, we began to function as one unit. The quote I always use at work is *"Teamwork makes the dream work."* If you are not working together, it's hard to discuss tough issues like finances and raising your children. Do you believe your husband has found a rare jewel in you?

> He who finds a wife finds a good thing,
>   And obtains favor from the Lord.
>
> Proverbs 18:22

Single women get caught up trying to "find a man" because of their age, and the pressure of society. They lose sight of working on becoming a good wife. It will be more beneficial if you begin working on being a wife, then trying to figure it out after the wedding.

When you accept Jesus as your Lord and Savior and believe that he died and rose, then you become heirs with him.

> The Spirit Himself testifies with our spirit that we are children of God, and if children, heirs also, heirs of God and fellow heirs with Christ, if indeed we suffer with Him so that we may also be glorified with Him.
>
> -Romans 8:16-17

When you marry a person who is born again, you two become joint heirs together. Spiritually, the husband and wife are on the same level, but domestically the husband is the headship. The man has to consider his wife as a child of God, his sister. There is no partiality when God gives out judgment.

LOVING & PEACEFUL

Pondering those two words, I wonder if my husband considers our home to be loving and peaceful. I desire my husband to feel loved when he comes home, but do I exhibit this characteristic, or do I allow my emotions to overtake me?

> Can two walk together, except they be agreed?
>
> Amos 3:3

If you and your spouse are not communicating on the same level, it will be impossible to agree. The Scripture reminds me of the game, three-legged race. While someone is tying the legs together, the teammates should be devising a plan on how they will get to the finish line. If they didn't communicate, they would run in different directions, and both will fall. In marriage when you are not communicating effectively, and creating a loving and peaceful home, it will fall. Eventually, strife will build up, and you will start thinking the *grass is greener on the other side*. In truth, the grass is not greener; if you take the time to maintain yours, it will be the best looking grass in the neighborhood.

The grass is NOT greener

As part of my husband's nonprofit, we facilitate goal-setting classes. The purpose of these classes is to hold people accountable for their short and long-term goals. Many single women's goal is to get married. As women, you should evaluate if this has been your goal year after year. At some point, you should seek God asking him why your prayers are not being answered. Are you approachable? I have told several young ladies who desire to be married, that every guy who approaches them is not the enemy. Your desire is to marry someone who loves the Lord, but are you giving them an opportunity to show you? You have to be loving and peaceful in your singleness as well.

Trust in the LORD and do good; Dwell in the land
and cultivate faithfulness. Delight yourself in the
LORD; And He will give you the desires of your
heart. Commit your way to the LORD, Trust also in
Him, and He will do it....

-Psalm 37: 3-5

In your prayer time, ask God to reveal to you if you are trusting him, dwelling, and cultivating faithfulness. He will show you, and if you listen, these three principles are the keys to your prayers being answered.

ARE YOUR PRAYERS HINDERED

There have been more times than I want to count when David and I have gotten into arguments, went to work, and someone unexpectedly needed serious prayers. After that happened several times, David finally said, we need to make it right, so our prayers are not hindered.

When your husband makes decisions, but disregards his wife and doesn't seek forgiveness, ultimately his prayers are not answered. If he utilizes his wife and sees the value of her being a joint heir, the marriage will be successful.

As a husband, you have to remember to keep in mind that you are dealing with a child of God. Regardless of how she responds, you don't disrespect her.

He said to His disciples, "It is inevitable that stumbling blocks come, but woe to him through whom they come! "It would be better for him if a millstone were hung around his neck and he were thrown into the sea, than that he would cause one of these little ones to stumble.

-Luke 17:1-2

NO REPUTATION

Husbands, even in your authoritative state, consider those who are subject to your authority. Jesus is your advocate. Blessings are hidden in humility. Jesus made himself of no reputation. He couldn't usurp his authority, despite having just cause, because he knew the result he was to obtain.

But made himself of no reputation, and took upon him the form of a servant, and was made in the likeness of men.

-Philippians 2:7

If Jesus, the son of God, can take on the form of a servant, then why can't we? Understanding why it is important to crucifying your flesh will allow a wife to submit to her husband. As a wife, you want to be of no reputation. You cannot live for other's thoughts or opinions of you. Walk in grace and love, and remember this:

Wherefore laying aside all malice, and all guile, and hypocrisies, and envies, and all evil speakings,
As newborn babes, desire the sincere milk of the word, that ye may grow thereby:
If so be ye have tasted that the Lord is gracious.
Honour all men. Love the brotherhood. Fear God. Honour the king.
Servants, be subject to your masters with all fear; not only to the good and gentle, but also to the forward.
For this is thankworthy, if a man for conscience toward God endure grief, suffering wrongfully.

For what glory is it, if, when ye be buffeted for your faults, ye shall take it patiently? but if, when ye do well, and suffer for it, ye take it patiently, this is acceptable with God.

1 Peter 2: 1-3; 17-20

DIG DEEP

1. Could you and your spouse win a three-legged race?

   _____

   _____

2. Is your home loving and peaceful?

   _____

   _____

3. What are some things you can do to improve your teamwork skills?

   _____

   _____

   _____

4. Are your prayers being hindered?

   _____

   _____

5. What can you do to ensure you and your spouse don't go to bed angry?

   _____

   _____

PERSONAL PRAYER

Focus on living with no reputation.

_____

_____

_____

_____

_____

_____

_____

_____

_____

_____

_____

_____

_____

TO DO:

1. Start a Bible study in your home.
2. Pray together every morning

Chapter Seven

Proverbs 31 Woman

Who can find a virtuous woman?
-Proverbs 31:10

God has given us the tools we need as women to be the best wife he has intended us to be. In Proverbs 31:10-31, God is clear on the characteristics of a virtuous woman. I have read this many times, but it wasn't until recently that I fully understood this is what my husband *needs* for us to have a successful marriage. Even in your singleness, you should be reading this proverb and constantly examining yourself.

Who can find a virtuous woman? For her price is far above rubies.

-Proverbs 31:10

Rubies are the second hardest mineral in existence after diamonds and the oldest gemstones known to man. When you know your value, you will begin to carry yourself differently, and not allow anyone to mistreat or disrespect you.

> He who finds a wife finds a good thing and obtains favor from the LORD.
>
> -Proverbs 18:22

It is not a women's duty to go out and find a husband. She will be acting outside the Word of God. A godly man wants to pursue a woman. He wants to win her over and obtain favor. You don't have to dress seductively or give up your virtue to keep him. A Godly man will honor you, and want to preserve intimacy until marriage.

> The heart of her husband doth safely trust in her, so that he shall have no need of spoil. She will do him good and not evil all the days of her life.
>
> -Proverbs 31:11, 12

It is your business to please your husband. Think of it as your job. When you are hired, employers provide you the necessary skills to do the job. It is up to you to perfect yourself in that position. Use the skills God has provided, he will reveal the mind and heart of your husband so you can please and submit to him.

A virtuous woman conducts herself with all respect. She does not embarrass him in public. He can be relaxed knowing she will represent him with prudence. He has confidence in her even when he is away. He doesn't worry or has to be jealous. As a wife, you should honor his counsel and his family. It should not be any separation between your family and his. Families should come together and get along with no strife.

When David and I were dating, we had our parents meet. We believed it was important for our families to know each other and get along. To this date, our families can come together and have a genuine love for each other.

She seeketh wool, and flax, and worketh willingly with her hands. She is like the merchants' ships; she bringeth her food from afar.

-Proverbs 31:13, 14

A virtuous woman is not lazy. Whether she is a stay-at-home wife or works outside the home, you have a responsibility to ensure your home is kept clean, and to provide the necessary food for your family. I work full-time and have young children, who require a lot of my attention. This does not excuse me from cleaning my house, or ensuring we have food to cook. My husband doesn't expect the home to be spotless every day, especially with a one- and four-year-old, but tidy.

As a husband, you want to assist your wife in these duties. If she is bathing the kids or helping with homework, offer to cook. If she is washing dishes, offer to sweep or mop. Remember you are a team, and teammates work together to make it work.

She riseth also while it is yet night, and giveth meat to her household, and a portion to her maidens.
Proverbs 31:15

Many women say they are not "a morning person." When you have a husband and children, you should wake up and make sure the necessary preparations are made for your family. Having two kids, I have to ensure my children's school clothes are washed and prepared before going to bed. I don't cook breakfast during the week, but every morning I make certain my kids have eaten breakfast, and their bags are prepared and ready for the day.

As a wife, you are also using this time to pray for your family and your home. Use this as your devotion time. Remember, your relationship with Christ doesn't stop because you are married.

She considereth a field, and buyeth it: with the fruit of her hands she planteth a vineyard.
She girdeth her loins with strength, and strengtheneth her arms.

-Proverbs 31:16, 17

A virtuous woman is a business lady. Sometimes a woman has to work to assist with household finances. Be creative. If your desire is to be home with your children, then create revenue while at home. Seek God, and allow him to direct you. You are strong; while sometimes finances can be stressful in a marriage, don't allow it to rule over your heart. Make a smart decision together, and allow the peace of God to have the final authority.

She perceiveth that her merchandise is good: her candle goeth not out by the night. She layeth her hands to the spindle, and her hands hold the distaff. She stretcheth out her hand to the poor; yea, she reacheth forth her hands to the needy.

-Proverbs 31: 18-20

A virtuous woman should want to look back at her labor from rising early, and going to bed late worth the sacrifice. Even if you never receive praises from your husband, your priority, next to God, is your family. It does me good when my husband recognizes the small efforts. Somedays I have felt not appreciated, but when I decided to go before God and tell my husband, it never ended well. I have found that when I don't say anything, regardless of my feelings at the time, my husband would come back with an appreciation I knew that only God had put on his heart.

Sometimes God blesses us with more than enough. I would consider myself to be extremely blessed. The majority of my home was furnished by my family. I don't mind giving away clothes and furniture because I know God will give it back. With my husband's nonprofit, we facilitate workshops on weeknights. It is a sacrifice to work eight hours, and then give another three hours to people other than your family. We do it because we know God called us to do this work, and we know he will bless us. My pastor uses the scripture in 1 Samuel 15:22, "Obedience is better than sacrifice." I don't want to do anything to hinder God's blessing.

She is not afraid of the snow for her household: for all
her household are clothed with scarlet. She maketh
herself coverings of tapestry; her clothing is silk and
purple.

-Proverbs 31: 21, 22

Here is your reward for all your hard work.
When you have made the sacrifices, God will
honor you. Your family will have nice clothing,
and no worries about their next meal. He will
reward you with the finest clothing that even
your husband will be proud. What women
doesn't want to look nice? I am not a "high-
heels, dress-wearing" type of girl. My silk and
purple are a new pair of tennis shoes, and an
outfit to match. Don't go on your accord and
create debt by using credit to buy your "silk and
purple." Debt creates tension and possibly a
financial setback. Whatever your preference is,
allow God to bless you with it.

Her husband is known in the gates, when he sitteth
among the elders of the land.

-Proverbs 31: 24

As a wife, you want to build up your husband. You want to respect him in the home, and in public. His reputation starts with you, a virtuous woman. Support him, love him, and encourage him. If you tear him down with negativity, how can he lead effectively? When you made a decision to marry him, you decided to follow his lead.

She maketh fine linen, and selleth it; and delivereth girdles unto the merchant. Strength and honour are her clothing; and she shall rejoice in time to come.
-Proverbs 31:24, 25

This scripture again speaks to the woman's ability to be an entrepreneur. She will team up with her husband to ensure a well-cared for home. Women who fear the Lord will be displayed. Your inward character is your clothing. When you spend time with God, he will give you the wisdom and confidence needed for being a wife and mother. When hard times come, you will be able to recognize it, handle it with confidence, and rejoice.

She opened her mouth with wisdom; and in her tongue
is the law of kindness. She looked well to the ways of
her household, and eateth not the bread of idleness.

-Proverbs 31: 26, 27

As a godly wife, you don't want to tear
down your husband or children. Your words
should be used for edification. You shouldn't
be gossiping. When you chastise your children,
it's for instruction and guidance. Take care your
home, husband, and children. Find those quiet
moments to spend with God. In the times we
are in, social media has taken a lot of time away
from real conversations in the home. If you can
find time to look at everyone's "status," then
you have time to get a status update from God.
When you seek him, he will honor his Word.

Her children arise up, and call her blessed; her husband
also. And he praiseth her. Many daughters have done
virtuously, but thou excellest them all.
Favour is deceitful, and beauty is vain: but a woman
that feareth the Lord, she shall be praised. Give her of

the fruit of her hands; and let her own works praise her in the gates.

-Proverbs 31: 28-31

When you exhibit the love of Christ to your husband and children, you will be praised. They will respect and honor you. Someone is always watching you; being an example to younger women will empower them to be virtuous. Don't be the person talking about being a virtuous woman; be a living witness. People should be encouraged to get married, not fearful of what they have seen or experience.

.........⟨♪⟩.........

I was watching *The Dark Knight Rises* during the Thanksgiving break and got a revelation. In the movie, Batman was injured and thrown into a well-like prison where escape was nearly impossible. After months of recovering, he begin attempting his escape. To escape, he had to jump from one side of the well to a small ledge. To protect himself, he tied himself to a rope and attempted the jump.

After being unsuccessful several times, he realized that being tied down was holding him from his victory. It wasn't until he utilized faith, was he able to escape.

Being submissive to your husband as unto the Lord is not about losing yourself. Opportunity only benefits the prepared mind. Are you prepared to do as God commanded? Are you prepared to die to self, and gain all power in humility by calling him lord? Try God at his Word. It will not return to you void.

~God Bless

Notes

Chapter One:

Submission is a Command

1. A. J. Darkholme as quoted in *Rise of the Morningstar,* compiled by http://www.goodreads.com/quotes/tag/submission. October 2015.

2. Submission retrieved from Merriam-Webster. October 2015

3. Shifting your Perspective. Retrieved from http://www.truthpizza.org/logic/perspect.htm. October 2015

Chapter Two:

Win without Words

1. Vince Lombardi as quoted, complied by http://www.brainyquote.com/quotes/authors/v/vince_lombardi.html. October 2015.

2. David E. Pratte. *Meekness and Humility: God's Cure for Pride, Haughtiness, and Egotism.* http://www.gospelway.com/christianlife/meekness.php. 2005

3. Andrew Murray. *Humility.* First Electronic Edition. September 2012

Chapter Three:
True beauty of a godly woman

1. Audrey Hepburn as quoted, compiled by http://www.brainyquote.com/quotes/topics/topic _beauty.html. October 2015

2. David Guzik commentary. Study guide for 1 Peter 3. Retrieved from www.blueletterbible.org

Chapter Four:
Sarah obeyed Abraham

1. James Faust as quoted, complied by http://brainyquotes.com/quotes/keywords/obide nce.html. November 2015

2. What does the bible say about Obedience? Retrieved from http://www.gotquestions.org/Bible-obedience.html. November 2015

3. All about God. *Marital Intimacy.* Retrieved from http://www.allaboutgod.com/marital-intimacy.htm. November 2015

Chapter Five:
Giving honor to the Wife

1. Calvin Coolidge as quoted, complied by http://www.brainyquote.com/quotes/keywords/honor.html. November 2015

Chapter Six:
Heirs Together

1. Henry Ford as quoted, complied by http://www.brainyquote.com/quotes/quotes/h/henryford121997.html. November 2015

About the Author

Wendy Magee has been married to David Magee Jr. for eight years and is the proud mother of two beautiful children Kaleb (4) and Kyrie (1). Wendy is currently the Director of Operations for CASA Jefferson, Inc. She is an ordained Minister and attends Mount Carmel Ministries under the leadership of Apostle Arthal Thomas Sr.

Wendy has served as a Youth Leader and led a young women's ministry with her sister-in-law. She also serves as the Treasurer for her husband's non-profit organization, H.Y.P.E.

She currently resides in New Orleans, LA. Wendy believes none of this would be possible without obeying God's command by submitting and supporting her husband mission.

www.ingramcontent.com/pod-product-compliance
Lightning Source LLC
Chambersburg PA
CBHW031523040426
42445CB00009B/364